SO-BED-966

SAND DUNES

by Ellen Fuller

SCHOOL PUBLISHERS

Cover, ©Carsten Peter/National Geographic/Getty Images; p.4–5, ©F. Lukasseck/Masterfile; p.6-7, ©Jeff Hunter/The Image Bank/Getty Images; p.8-9, ©Adam Jones/Visuals Unlimited/Getty Images; p.10–11, ©COLIN MONTEATH/HEDGEHOG HOUSE/Minden Pictures; p.12, ©Bernd Kohlhas/zefa/Corbis; p.13, ©George Steinmetz/Corbis; p.14, ©Robert Holmes/Corbis.

Cartography, p.3, Joe LeMonnier

Copyright © by Harcourt, Inc.

All rights reserved. No part of this publication may be reproduced or transmitted in any form or by any means, electronic or mechanical, including photocopy, recording, or any information storage and retrieval system, without permission in writing from the publisher.

Requests for permission to make copies of any part of the work should be addressed to School Permissions and Copyrights, Harcourt, Inc., 6277 Sea Harbor Drive, Orlando, Florida 32887 6777. Fax: 407-345-2418.

HARCOURT and the Harcourt Logo are trademarks of Harcourt, Inc., registered in the United States of America and/or other jurisdictions.

Printed in China

ISBN 10: 0-15-350789-6
ISBN 13: 978-0-15-350789-2

Ordering Options
ISBN 10: 0-15-350601-6 (Grade 4 On-Level Collection)
ISBN 13: 978-0-15-350601-7 (Grade 4 On-Level Collection)
ISBN 10: 0-15-357926-9 (package of 5)
ISBN 13: 978-0-15-357926-4 (package of 5)

If you have received these materials as examination copies free of charge, Harcourt School Publishers retains title to the materials and they may not be resold. Resale of examination copies is strictly prohibited and is illegal.

Possession of this publication in print format does not entitle users to convert this publication, or any portion of it, into electronic format.

4 5 6 7 8 9 10 0940 12 11 10 09

Hiking is very popular at the Guadalupe-Nipomo Dunes National Wildlife Refuge. This beautiful area is on the California coast. It is about midway between the cities of Los Angeles and San Francisco. Hikers come to the area to observe its many beautiful sand dunes.

Like mountains, dunes are hilly landforms that rise up from the Earth's surface. Dunes and mountains, however, form in very different ways. The movements of the Earth's crust form some mountains. Erupting volcanoes form other mountains. Dunes are formed much more simply than mountains.

Mountains often take millions of years to form. Dunes, however, can take shape in a matter of weeks. Mountains are made of rock. Dunes are almost always made up of simple sand. In fact, all it really takes to make a dune is a supply of sand and a constant wind or breeze. Photographs from space reveal that dunes even form on the planet Mars.

Dunes are often found on beaches and in deserts. That is because both of these places have the key ingredient needed to make a dune: sand.

Most sand is made up of the mineral called quartz. Quartz is not weathered or broken down very easily. While other kinds of minerals are washed away, the quartz remains.

Over millions of years, the quartz builds up and condenses. After a while some areas, such as deserts, have a lot of quartz—and so they also have a lot of sand.

The sand along coasts and beaches usually comes from rivers and streams. These waterways carry the sand to the sea or ocean. Then currents gradually move the sand farther into the water. Waves then wash the sand onto the shore again.

A dune first begins to form when a strong wind blows and picks up grains of sand. If the sand grains are too large or heavy, the wind will not be able to pick them up. Because of this, almost all dunes are made from small grains of sand. One exception is along the coast of Peru, in South America. The winds there are so strong that they are able to pick up and carry small pebbles. Therefore, the dunes on the coast of Peru are made up of pebbles and sand. After the wind picks up the sand, it blows it along, usually close to the ground.

Along a coastline, the sand may hit something and stop. For example, the sand may run into a piece of driftwood or a plant. As more sand blows, it hits that same barrier and falls to the ground. Over time, a small pile of sand builds up in that spot. This pile stops more sand from blowing. This repeats over and over. The sand pile grows larger and larger until it finally forms a dune.

In deserts, the blowing sand often stops when it comes to a low spot in the ground. More blowing sand hits the sand in that low spot and also stops. This process repeats itself. The pile of sand grows larger and larger, and a dune is created.

In time, the dune takes the shape of a hill. The front of the dune, where the wind hits it, rises little by little. The back of the dune is steeper. When more sand blows on the dune, the sand rides up the front of the dune. Then, it goes over the edge at the top, and immediately falls down the steep back of the dune.

The unusual shape of the dune allows these hills to actually move. Suppose a stable sand dune is resting along a coastline. The wind begins to blow. It takes sand from the front of the dune and carries it over to the back of the dune.

More sand from the front is blown to the back. As this continues, the dune slowly inches forward along the ground. Some dunes in California move more than 70 feet (21.3 m) per year. Dunes in Egypt have moved over 300 feet (91.4 m) in one year!

Dunes do not move when they are covered with plants. This is because the roots of plants help hold the sand in place. Therefore, many dunes on the coast last a long time. In fact, some dunes in California are more than 18,000 years old. Dunes that do not have plants to hold them in place can slowly shrink, or contract.

One plant is very efficient at keeping dunes from moving. It is called European beach grass. When sand blows onto these plants and buries them, the plants quickly grow a new root or shoot. These roots or shoots block more sand from moving. So, the dune is able to survive.

A lot of European beach grass was planted on California dunes in the 1930s. This was done to make them stable and keep them from blowing away. Even stable dunes, though, can be wrecked by strong storms. In California, storms during the winter often erode sand from the dunes. The sand is blown into the depths of the Pacific Ocean. In the summer, the sand washes back on shore and is blown onto the dunes again.

Dunes on the coast usually appear in sets of two or three. They run next to each other. The dunes also run directly along the ocean. The youngest dunes are the ones closest to the shore. The oldest dunes are the ones that are the farthest away from the shore.

The oldest dunes are often covered with trees and grass. There is rich soil on the surface of the dunes. This helps many plants grow. As more and more plants grow on these dunes, wildlife will come. Over the years the dunes may become home to birds, insects, and animals. The plants covering old dunes keep them from being destroyed.

Star dunes are perhaps the most beautiful dunes in the world. They look like a starfish, with long arms coming out from the center. Star dunes have three or more of these "arms." Star dunes form in deserts where winds blow from several different directions. The center of a star dune has a triangle shape and can grow quite tall. Star dunes in China's Badain Jaran Desert can sometimes grow to be over 1,500 feet (457 m) tall! Some scientists think they are the tallest dunes on earth.

The coast of California has twenty-seven different groups of dunes. Large dune areas are found near San Diego Bay, Humboldt Bay, and Guadalupe-Nipomo. The largest area of dunes in California is found by the Monterey Bay, near the city of Monterey.

Unfortunately, more dunes in California are being destroyed and weakened than are being created. One reason is dams. Dams stop the flow of sand down rivers. So, there is less sand to be deposited into the ocean and less sand to be blown up onto the dunes. Also, people ride on the dunes in vehicles or on horses. This often damages the plants that live on dunes. Without plants, dunes may blow away and disappear.

Think Critically

1. How do plants affect dunes?

2. What is needed to form star dunes?

3. What problem is discussed in this book?

4. What are dunes made of?

5. What do you think is the most important thing you read in this book?

 Science

Dune Diagram This book tells about some kinds of sand dunes. Look in a science book or on the Internet for other types of dunes. Find out what other dunes look like and how they are formed. Draw a diagram of another kind of dune.

 School-Home Connection Discuss this book with a family member. Talk about what humans can do to help preserve dunes.

Word Count: 1,173 (1,184)